0808829

The Sense of Hearing

ELAINE LANDAU

Children's Press®
An Imprint of Scholastic Inc.
New York Toronto London Auckland Sydney
Mexico City New Delhi Hong Kong
Danbury, Connecticut

Content Consultant

Lawrence J. Cheskin, M.D.
Johns Hopkins Bloomberg School of Public Health
Baltimore, MD

Library of Congress Cataloging-in-Publication Data

Landau, Elaine.
  The sense of hearing / by Elaine Landau.
      p. cm. -- (A true book)
  Includes index.
      ISBN-13: 978-0-531-16870-7 (lib. bdg.)
            978-0-531-21832-7 (pbk.)
      ISBN-10: 0-531-16870-0 (lib. bdg.)
            0-531-21832-5 (pbk.)

1. Hearing--Juvenile literature. I. Title.

  QP462.2.L36 2008
  612.8'5--dc22   2007048048

Produced by Weldon Owen Education Inc.

1 2 3 4 5 6 7 8 9 10 R 18 17 16 15 14 13 12 11 10 09

Find the Truth!

Everything you are about to read is true *except* for one of the sentences on this page.

Which one is **TRUE**?

T or F   Dogs are born with better hearing than humans.

T or F   Sound waves travel through water faster than they travel through air.

Find the answers in this book.

Contents

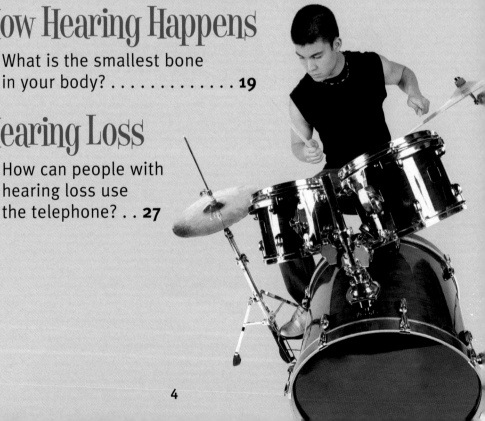

If you want to hear better, cup your hand behind your ear.

THE **BIG** TRUTH!

Talking Hands

5 Protecting Your Hearing

CHAPTER 1

Sounds Surround You

BEEP-BEEP-BEEP! The alarm clock wakes you up. Minutes later, a voice calls you to breakfast. POP! Your toast is ready. HONK-HONK! There's your ride to school. "Don't forget your coat!" calls Dad.

From the moment we wake up, we hear sounds. Most of us depend on our hearing every day.

 Even in noisy places, you can pick out different sounds happening at the same time.

Experiencing Sound

Hearing is one of the five senses. The others are sight, smell, touch, and taste. Like the other senses, hearing gives you information about your surroundings.

If you can hear, most of your experiences involve hearing. For example, when you look at ocean waves, you also hear them crash on the shore. Your sense of hearing helps you know where objects are in relation to you. It helps you understand the world around you.

Hearing enables us to communicate with each other.

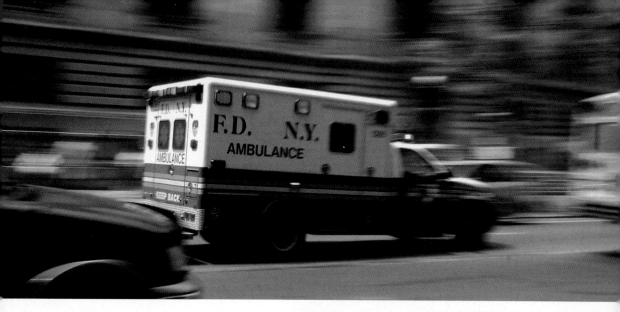

Sirens and alarms alert us to situations that may be dangerous.

Hearing the World

Your hearing is important to your safety. The sound of a smoke alarm or a car horn is a warning. At some crosswalks, a beep tells you it's safe to walk.

Hearing connects you to the world. A bell signals the start and end of the school day. When you hear the ring of a phone or a doorbell, you answer it. Even as you read this, you are probably reacting to all kinds of sounds around you.

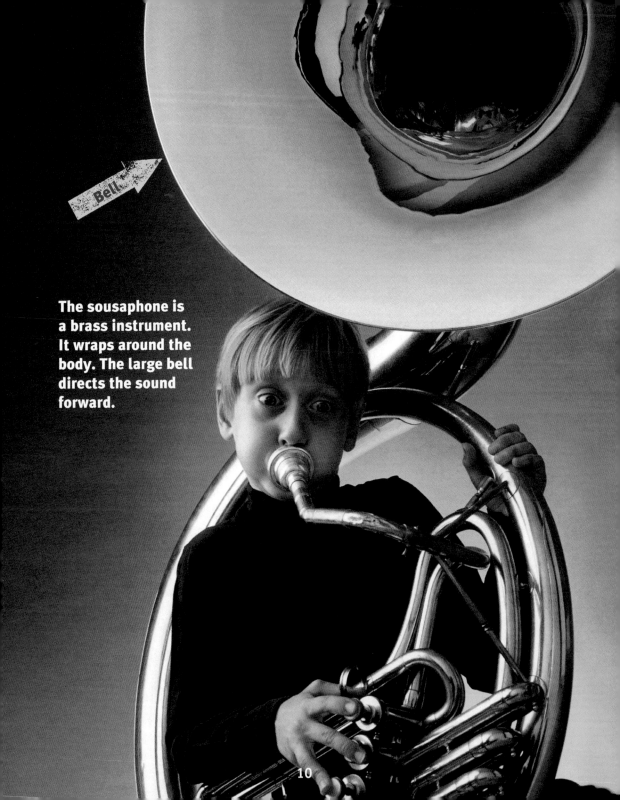

Bell

The sousaphone is
a brass instrument.
It wraps around the
body. The large bell
directs the sound
forward.

10

CHAPTER 2

What Is Sound?

Whether it's a whisper or an exploding firecracker, every sound is caused by **vibrations**. Vibrations are set off by motion. What is in motion may be a falling leaf or a mouth blowing into a brass instrument. Either way, vibrations are produced and travel through the air. If they are picked up by your ears, you hear a sound.

To play a brass instrument, you blow air through your lips into the mouthpiece. This vibration is called "buzzing."

Good Vibrations

Vibrations travel in the form of waves. Most of the sound waves we hear travel through the air, which is a gas. Sound waves also move through solids and liquids to reach our ears. Sound actually travels fastest through solids and slowest through gases.

The saying "keep an ear to the ground" means to listen for something.

Sounds travel faster through solid earth than through air. Some Native Americans used to place an ear to the ground to hear if people, horses, or buffalo were approaching.

In outer space, an astronaut cannot hear any sounds outside of his or her space suit.

No Vibrations

Vibrating air allows you to hear a friend speak from across a room. But what if you and your friend were on the moon? You would not be able to hear each other there. That's because there is no air in outer space, so there is nothing for sound to travel through. When astronauts are in outer space, they use radio equipment to talk to one another.

Get on the Wavelength

The speed of a sound wave's vibrations determines a sound's **pitch**. Fast vibrations make high-pitched sounds, like those of a squeaky voice or a violin. Slower vibrations produce low-pitched sounds, like those of a deep voice or a tuba. Pitch is measured by the number of sound waves per second. This is called **frequency**. The more vibrations, the higher the frequency and the higher the pitch. Frequency is counted in Hertz (Hz). Humans hear sounds with a frequency of 20 to 20,000 Hz.

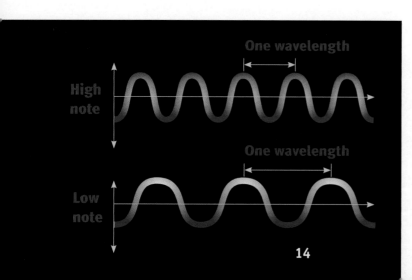

Scientists draw sound waves as wavy lines. High sounds have shorter wavelengths than low sounds do. The waves of high sounds also have a higher frequency.

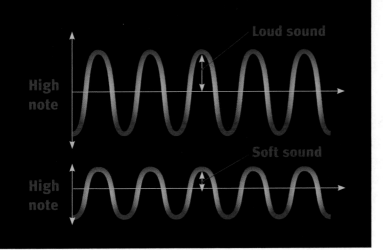

Loud sound

High note

Soft sound

High note

These wavelengths have the same frequency, but one is louder than the other. The top wavelength has more power.

The Power of Sound

Every sound possesses loudness, as well as pitch. This is known as the power, or **intensity**, of a sound. Power is measured in decibels (dB). A measure of 0 dB is near-total silence. A sound 10 times more powerful is 10 dB. A sound 100 times more powerful than one of 0 dB is 20 dB.

The decibel was named in honor of Alexander Graham Bell. He invented the telephone.

Measures of Some Common Sounds

Any sound over 85 dB can cause hearing loss. Exposure to a sound of 140 dB can instantly do permanent damage to your hearing.

Whispering
20 dB

Talking
60 dB

Blender
80 dB

Lawn mower
100 dB

Speeding train
110 dB

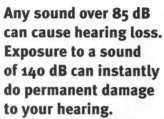

Rock concert
120 dB

Jet engines at takeoff
140 dB

Ocean Sounds

You may think that the ocean is a silent, watery world. However, it is really very noisy. Whales and dolphins communicate with one another with chirps and whistles. They also use sound to find food. They make a sound and listen to its echo as it bounces off objects in the ocean. This is called echolocation. Some fish make noises either to attract a mate or to scare away predators. Sea lions roar underwater. Some shrimp produce loudly bursting air bubbles as they snap their claws. The blue whale is the loudest animal on Earth. Its very low-frequency sound can reach more than 180 dB. Dolphins have one of the best senses of hearing among animals.

Dolphins

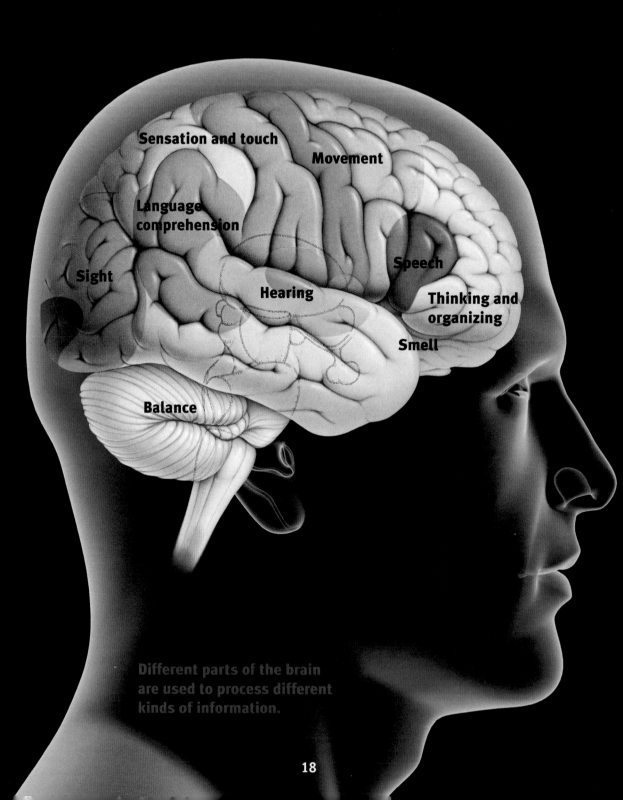

Sensation and touch

Movement

Language comprehension

Sight

Speech

Hearing

Thinking and organizing

Smell

Balance

Different parts of the brain are used to process different kinds of information.

18

CHAPTER 3

How Hearing Happens

Most people will say they hear with their ears. They are only partly right. Hearing begins with your ears, but there is a lot more to it. The brain plays an important part in how you hear, as well.

Dogs are born deaf. They begin to hear when they are about 12 days old.

Ear Control

You have one ear on each side of your head.
This helps your brain locate the direction a sound
is coming from. Then you can turn your head
in that direction to better hear the sound.

All of this happens because your ear and your
brain work together to process sound information.
Sound is received and carried through
the three main parts of the ear:
the outer ear, the middle ear,
and the inner ear.

Some animals, such as
rabbits and horses, can
turn their entire outer ears
in the direction from which
a sound is coming. Strong
muscles attach their outer
ears to their head.

On the Outside

The outer ear is also known as the earflap or **pinna**. It is the part of the ear you can see. The outer ear is somewhat cup-shaped. This makes it well suited to catching sound waves. It is made of tough, bendable tissue called cartilage.

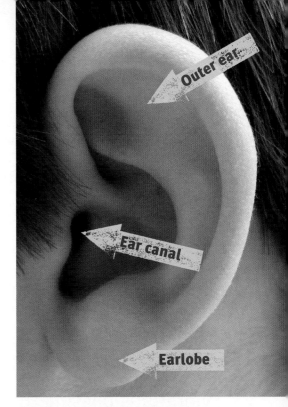

Earwax is produced in the ear canal. Its job is to prevent damage to the eardrum by trapping dirt and other particles.

Sound waves that are caught by the outer ear are funneled into the ear canal. The canal is about one inch (2.5 centimeters) long. It leads to a thin, round **membrane** called the eardrum. This separates the outer ear from the middle ear.

In the Middle

The middle ear receives sound waves through the eardrum. The vibration of the eardrum causes the bones in the middle ear to vibrate. These bones are tiny—the entire middle ear is only about the size of a raisin! The three bones are called the hammer, anvil, and stirrup. They are linked together and they link the eardrum to the inner ear. Sound vibrations passing through the middle ear are made bigger, or **amplified**.

The middle ear is also connected to the back of the throat by a passageway called the eustachian (yoo-STAY-shuhn) tube. This tube allows air to reach the middle ear. The tube opens when you open your mouth, swallow, yawn, or blow your nose. This action equalizes the air pressure on either side of the eardrum.

Inside the Ear

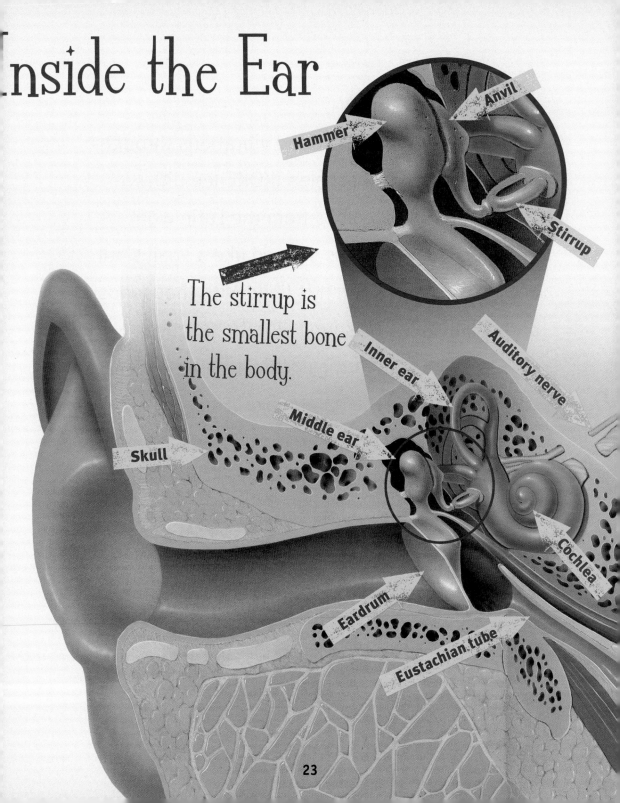

The stirrup is the smallest bone in the body.

Hammer

Anvil

Stirrup

Inner ear

Auditory nerve

Middle ear

Skull

Cochlea

Eardrum

Eustachian tube

The Inside Story

The inner ear receives sound vibrations through an organ called the cochlea (KOKE-lee-uh). The word *cochlea* comes from the Latin word for snail. The cochlea is shaped like a snail shell and is filled with fluid. It is lined with thousands of tiny hair cells. As sound vibrations move through the cochlear fluid, they make the hairs move. The hair cells then turn the vibrations into electrical signals, or impulses. These signals travel to the brain along the **auditory** nerve.

Loud sounds make more hair cells move than soft sounds do. This makes the auditory nerve send more impulses to the brain.

A cricket's hearing organs are on its front legs.

Brain Power

The brain works like a central computer. Specific parts of the brain are set up to receive and decode information from each of the senses. The brain sorts out auditory signals so that you are able to hear the differences among speech, music, animal noises, and other sounds.

Your brain is at work twenty-four hours a day. It processes sounds even while you are asleep. If a sound is out of the ordinary, such as a crying baby or an alarm clock, your brain sends signals that wake you up in response to the sound.

It is important for babies and young children to get their ears checked and their hearing tested.

CHAPTER 4

Hearing Loss

It's easy to take your hearing for granted. Most people are born with hearing. However, about three out of every one thousand babies are born with some degree of hearing loss. In other cases, hearing loss develops later in life.

Octopuses have excellent eyesight, but they have no hearing organs. They are completely deaf.

Birth and Beyond

Hearing loss is the most common birth defect. Sometimes parts of the outer ear or middle ear have not formed properly. Surgeons may be able to replace some of these parts. However, defects of the inner ear cannot be repaired.

After birth, a severe infection or a head injury can result in hearing loss. Sudden explosive sounds or exposure to very loud noises over a long period can also damage hearing.

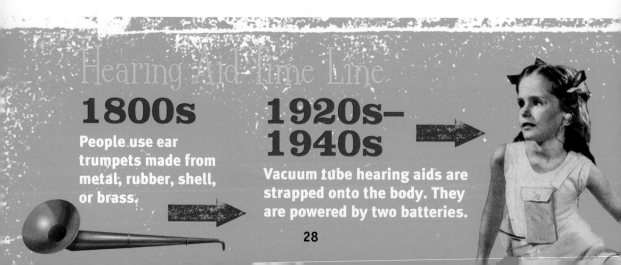

Hearing Aid Time Line

1800s

People use ear trumpets made from metal, rubber, shell, or brass.

1920s–1940s

Vacuum tube hearing aids are strapped onto the body. They are powered by two batteries.

Seeing a Specialist

A person who may have hearing loss needs to see an **audiologist** (aw-dee-OL-uh-jist). This is someone trained to identify hearing loss and suggest ways to help the person. Treatment for hearing loss varies. It depends on the type of hearing loss and how severe it is.

Sometimes medicine, an operation, or a hearing aid is needed. A hearing aid is a device used to amplify sounds. It is like a tiny loudspeaker. A hearing aid fits in or behind the ear.

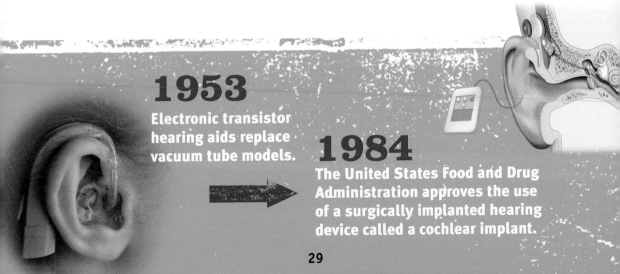

1953
Electronic transistor hearing aids replace vacuum tube models.

1984
The United States Food and Drug Administration approves the use of a surgically implanted hearing device called a cochlear implant.

Bringing Hearing Back

Hearing aids are not the answer for everyone who has hearing loss. A **cochlear implant** is an electronic device that is sometimes called a "bionic ear." This is because it takes over most of the hearing jobs of the ear.

A cochlear implant has several parts. An external microphone, placed behind the outer ear, picks up sounds. The microphone sends the sounds to an external transmitter. Just beneath the transmitter, under the skin, is the receiver. This part is implanted in the bone of the skull. It is where the sound signals are converted into electrical impulses. The impulses travel to the cochlea along a tiny cable. **Electrodes** inserted into the cochlea receive these electrical impulses. They transfer them to the auditory nerve.

From that point on, the "sound" message travels to the brain as if it had gone through the standard hearing process.

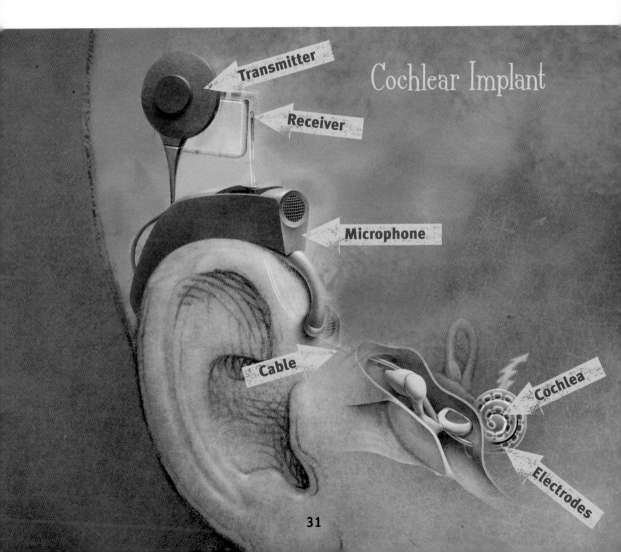

Cochlear Implant

Transmitter

Receiver

Microphone

Cable

Cochlea

Electrodes

Speaking With Your Hands

Young people who are deaf or have severe hearing loss often attend special schools or special classes in a public school. In these classes, students acquire skills to help them communicate and function in daily life.

One skill they work on is speaking. People who have never heard speech often have difficulty reproducing its sounds. Students work with a speech therapist to learn how to form the sounds of speech. They may also learn how to read lips. This helps them take part in conversations at school. Sign language is another important skill. This system uses hand signs, body movements, and facial expressions to show ideas, words, or letters. People who are deaf and their families often communicate using sign language.

Sign language offers people who are deaf an important way to communicate.

Technology Rules

Many people who are hearing **impaired** use the latest technology to help them communicate. A telecommunication display device (TDD) is a telephone with a keyboard and a screen. Instead of talking on the phone, people using a TDD send and receive typed messages.

Some TV shows, movies, and DVDs are now available with captions for the hearing impaired.

Captions on the bottom of the screen display what is being said.

A TDD allows the hearing impaired to have a conversation on the phone.

Hearing Dogs

Have you ever seen a guide dog helping a person who cannot see? People who are deaf or hearing impaired sometimes have the help of dogs also. Hearing dogs assist their owners by alerting them to important sounds around them. These include smoke alarms, telephones, doorbells, oven timers, and alarm clocks. Some dogs are trained to react to a baby's cry. Others are trained to listen for possible intruders.

Hands Up

ASL includes hand signs for common words. For example, for "thank you," you touch the lips with the fingertips of one hand. They you move the hand down until the palm is facing up.

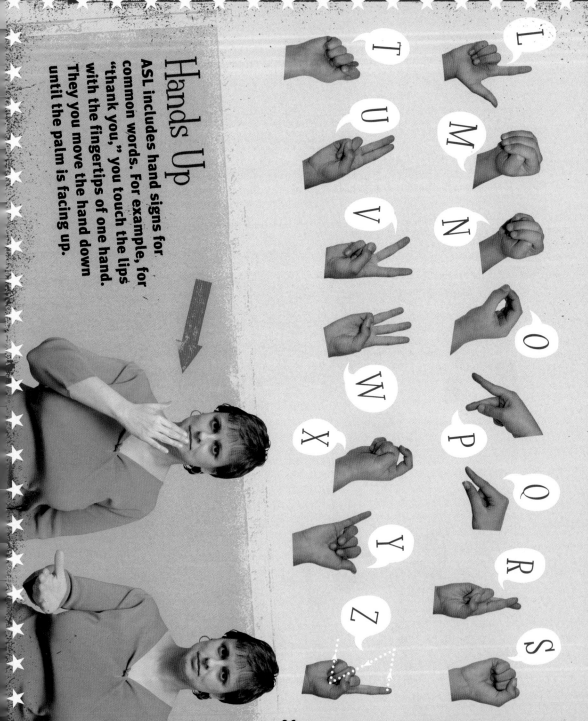

36

Talking Hands

Is it possible to "talk" without speaking? It is, if you use sign language. Different countries have their own versions of sign language. They all use hand gestures to express words and letters. In the United States, people learn American Sign Language (ASL).

Fine Fingers

ASL finger spelling uses the fingers of one hand to make signs for letters.

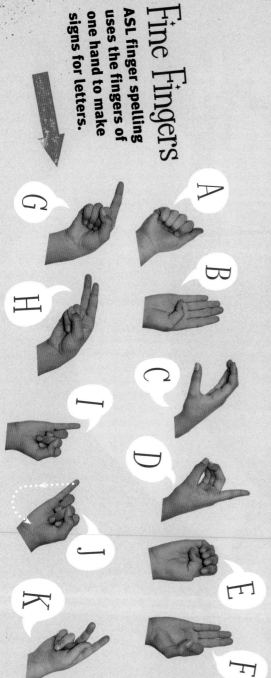

A B C D E F

G H I J K

Factory machinery, power saws, and even a hammer banging on a nail measure about 110 to 120 decibels.

CHAPTER 5

Protecting Your Hearing

The world is a noisy place. Sometimes loud sounds cannot be avoided. However, there are plenty of ways you can protect your hearing. Use your common sense and you can help maintain good hearing for all of your life.

← After five years on the job, the average carpenter has the same hearing as a 50-year-old person who doesn't work around noise.

Hearing Hazards

Some workplaces, such as airports, construction sites, and factories, are particularly noisy. Being exposed to loud noise over a long period of time may lead to ringing in the ears. This ringing may come and go, or it may be a continuous sound. It could be a high squeal or a low roar. Ongoing loud noise can destroy the delicate hair cells in your inner ear. Once damaged, these hair cells cannot be repaired.

Air-traffic ground crew must wear earmuffs to protect their hearing.

The noise level at some video arcades is about four times as loud as the noise level allowed in U.S. factories.

People can damage their hearing from going to loud concerts or noisy video arcades. Hearing loss can also happen simply from listening to music too loud with headphones on.

Play It Safe

Hearing loss from noise can be prevented. When wearing headphones, keep the music volume down. Play televisions and radios at a reasonable volume. If you go to a loud concert or arcade, wear earplugs. It's also a good idea to wear earmuffs when using a lawn mower. Your ability to hear enhances your experience of life. Your hearing is well worth protecting. ★

Try not to wear headphones for long periods of time. Limiting use to one hour a day is better for your hearing.

True Statistics

Speed of sound in the air: About 770 miles (1,239 kilometers) per hour

Number of Americans who have some hearing loss: About 30 million (10 percent of the population)

Number of Americans who have permanent hearing loss due to loud noise: About 10 million

Number of people in the United States who use American Sign Language: About 2 million

Number of people worldwide who have cochlear implants: About 60,000

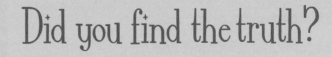

Did you find the truth?

F Dogs are born with better hearing than humans.

T Sound waves travel faster through water than they travel through air.

Resources

Books

Arnold, Caroline. *Did You Hear That? Animals With Super Hearing*. Watertown, MA: Charlesbridge Publications, 2001.

Ferguson, Beth. *The Ears* (Kaleidoscope). Tarrytown, NY: Benchmark Books, 2003.

Glaser, Jason. *Ear Infections* (First Facts). Mankato, MN: Capstone Press, 2007.

Hickman, Pamela. *How Animals Use Their Senses* (Kids Can Read). Toronto, ON: Kids Can Press, 2006.

Olien, Rebecca. *Hearing* (First Facts). Mankato, MN: Capstone Press, 2006.

Royston, Angela. *Healthy Ears and Eyes*. Chicago: Heinemann Library, 2003.

Simon, Seymour. *Eyes and Ears*. New York: HarperCollins, 2003.

Taylor-Butler, Christine. *The Nervous System* (A True Book: Health and the Human Body). Danbury, CT: Children's Press, 2008.

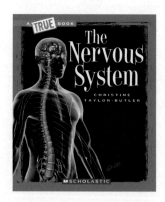

Tocci, Salvatore. *Experiments With Sound* (A True Book: Science Experiments). Danbury, CT: Children's Press, 2001.

Organizations and Web Sites

PBS Kids
http://pbskids.org/zoom/activities/sci/#sound
Follow the instructions to make musical instruments and create sounds. Send in the results of your experiments.

Enchanted Learning
www.enchantedlearning.com/subjects/anatomy/ear
Learn about the different parts of the ear.

Neuroscience for Kids
http://faculty.washington.edu/chudler/chhearing.html
Try some hearing experiments and get background information on how ears work.

Places to Visit

The Children's Museum of Virginia
221 High Street
Portsmouth, VA 23704
(757) 393 5258
www.childrensmuseumva.com/exhibits.html
See how sound waves travel, in the Simple Sonar exhibit.

Oregon Museum of Science and Industry
1945 SE Water Avenue
Portland, OR 97214-3354
(800) 955 6674
www.omsi.edu/visit/life
Learn about sound, in the Dangerous Decibels exhibit in the Life Science Hall.

Important Words

amplify – to make something louder or stronger

audiologist (aw-dee-OL-uh-jist) – a person who studies hearing disorders

auditory – having to do with hearing

cochlear implant – an electronic device that allows people with severe hearing loss to recognize some sounds

electrode – a point through which an electric current can flow into or out of a device

frequency – the number of times that something happens in a given time period

impaired – weakened or damaged

intensity – the strength or force of something

membrane – a very thin layer of tissue or skin that covers certain organs or cells

pinna – the visible part of the ear

pitch – the highness or lowness of a sound

vibration – a very fast back-and-forth movement

Index

Page numbers in **bold** indicate illustrations.

About the Author

Award-winning author Elaine Landau has a bachelor's degree from New York University and a master's degree in library and information science. She has written more than 300 nonfiction books for children and young adults.

Having spent many hours at the beach, Elaine Landau's favorite sounds are the sounds of the sea. She also enjoys hearing trained parrots speak.

Ms. Landau lives in Miami, Florida, with her husband and son. You can visit her at her Web site: www.elainelandau.com.

PHOTOGRAPHS: Big Stock Photo (p. 5; rock concert, p. 16; p. 17; p. 19; p. 35); Carol Hsu (p. 33; hands, pp. 36–37); Courtesy of Zenith Electronics LLC and Becker Medical Library, Washington University School of Medicine (girl, p. 28); Getty Images (p. 10); Ingram Image Library (p. 43); iStockphoto.com (back cover; pp. 3–4; pp. 8–9; train, blender, girls whispering, boys talking, p. 16; p. 17; head outline, p. 18; pp. 24–25; hearing aid, p. 29; ©Eliza Snow, p. 38; ©Doug Schneider, p. 42); ©Paul Kemp/www.sxc.hu (p. 20) ; Photodisc (p. 13); Photolibrary (p. 31; woman, p. 36; p. 41); Stock.Xchng (lawn mower, airplane, p. 16; p. 21); Tranz/Corbis (front cover; p. 6; p. 12; p. 15; brain, p. 18; p. 26; p. 34; p. 40)